# LIES, LOVE, and LIFE!

## TAKING BACK WHAT THE DEVIL THOUGHT HE STOLE FROM ME:

### *My Story!*

## ALICIA J. MORRISON

iUniverse, Inc.
Bloomington

**Lies, Love, and Life!**
**Taking Back What the Devil Thought**
**He Stole from Me: My Story!**

*iUniverse books may be ordered through booksellers or by contacting:*

*iUniverse*
*1663 Liberty Drive*
*Bloomington, IN 47403*
*www.iuniverse.com*
*1-800-Authors (1-800-288-4677)*

*ISBN: 978-1-4759-0181-8 (sc)*
*ISBN:978-1-4759-0182-5 (ebk)*

*Printed in the United States of America*

*iUniverse rev. date: 05/03/2012*

# DEDICATIONS and INSPIRATIONS

This book is first dedicated to Jesus Christ, who is the author and finisher of my faith, my grandmother, Marie Williams Morrison (deceased), and my Godmother, Joann Rivers. These two women with the help from above have been an inspiration to me even when I could not see my way. When the road seemed so long and the battle was not yet won, they have both inspired me to run on to see that there is a purpose for my going through. They have taught me that weeping may endure for a night, but joy comes in the morning. Even though my grandmother is deceased now, I love you dearly because you thought enough of me to take me in and raised me to be the God-fearing young woman I have grown to be. In addition, my Godmother, Mama, and thank you for being the spiritual guidance I needed to grow into the beautiful flower I have bloomed to be. Without the both of you watering, teaching, talking, and nurturing me, I would have withered up and died. Thank God for Jesus, and thank God for you two beautiful individuals that taught me everything about lies, love, and life. I love you both. Thank You!

# TABLE OF CONTENTS

# PREFACE

Writing has always been a strong point for me. I was in middle school when I found my love for writing. I would write great papers and poetry for assignments, but never would I have thought in a million years that I would write a book. I got older and God allowed me to learn what my talent was. I had been through so much in my life and I decided to put my talent to use. One day I was just sitting and thinking and God spoke to me and told me to go ahead and start writing my book. At first, I wasn't for sure if it was God speaking to me so I ignored His voice. About a month later, He spoke to me again but this time He gave me the title for the book. I then knew it was nobody but God. I obeyed this time and I began to write. I wrote most of it while I was at work where I had peace and quiet in the comfort of my own office. I would sat there for hours and write. Then I would type it into the computer that next day and then print each chapter out as I went along. I had some obstacles to distract me as I began to write the book. I would stop writing and then start back up. All together it took me about a year to finish writing the whole book. I think I could have been finished in less time, but the devil would send things and people to distract me because he knew the purpose God had for my life and the book and he didn't want me to execute what God had sat out for me to do. I finally finished the book in 2009. I gave it to someone I trust and let her pray over it and see what God told her about the book. I got pregnant and had my baby in 2010. After I had my baby, I decided it was time to start back up with my book. I let what other people said about me stop me from doing what God told me to do in the beginning. I prolonged it again because my family didn't think I should put the book out. Some said it was a get rich quick thing and then some said that it was wrong to tell the family business. Others were saying that I'm not going to make no money off the book because I was lying, and then there were some family memembers that said they were there for me and I had to do what I had to do. This was what God gave me to do and I that I had to go through these things in my life. I began to go to God in prayer and the bible tells me where two or three are gathered in His name; He will be in the midst. I trust God and He told me it was my season and time to do what He called me to do. I rededicated my life back to Him and decided to publish my book despite what the devil angels tried to say or do to me. The main purpose for my book is to help someone that may be going through what I have been through and to reassure them that if God brought me through all of this then He surely can bring them through whatever it is that they may be going through. I said this once and I will say it again, I would never do anything intentionally to ever hurt anyone especially family. I would never make up anything as horrible as the things that has happened to me about anyone. I finally realize after going through what I went through that there's purpose behind pain!

# CHAPTER 1

## *My Birth and Youth Years*

This is a true story about me, Alicia Jacquetta Morrison, better known by family and friends as Lucy. I was born on March 25, 1986. My mother gave birth to four other children besides me, and I am the oldest. I lived with my mother until I was about six years old. One day my mother and my step-dad left me and my other sibling's home by ourselves, and my step-dad's mother called the police and told them that we were home by ourselves. The police came and knocked on the door, and I was hesitant about opening the door, but I thought I would get in trouble by the police if I did not answer the door. I talked with the officer and he asked me how old was I and who else was in the house with me. I told him I was 6 years old and there were not any adults home. My step-dad's mother told the police that we were often left alone without adult supervision. She said that she called the police because she was concerned about our well-being, but in reality she did it because she did not like my mother being with her son. The police and DSS took us to foster homes. We all went to different homes.

My foster mother's name was Flora Washington. She was tall, brown skin complexion, and long thick hair. She was a good christian person, who took good care of me for about a year. I loved her for treating me like her own. I would like to tell what it was like living with my mother and step-dad. My mother was the type of woman, who very seldom said much, but she would look and we knew she meant business. She was not mean and I think more or less she did love us. She just was stuck with the wrong man. He made her do things that most husbands would not ask their wives to do. Like for instance, he would tell her to go to someone that they knew had money, and make like one of her children was sick and that they did not have any money to take them to the doctor or get the medicine. They would tell people sad stories that they knew people would fall for just to get money for marijuana and beer. They were so good at getting over on people, that some people would just give them because they felt sorry for us. I remember my siblings and I being so hungry and there was nothing in the hose to eat except bread and ketchup; so, this is what we ate a ketchup sandwich. I remember getting a beating from my stepdad for fixing my siblings a sandwich when they were hungry, and he caught me in the kitchen without permission. I remember my sibling and me sitting in a hot car with the windows rolled all the way up while my stepdad went inside somcone's house in the cool air. Just cruel I know, but we did have some good to go with the bad days. My whole family can sing. We come from a christian background of singers. I remember going to different churches singing. I remember practicing the night before going to church to sing, and we always listened to Tommy Ellison and the Five Singing Stars. I remember when we used to go see my grandmother, which was my mother's mother, Marie, who I will tell about later in the story. I loved going there because she fed us until we were so full we could not move. She used to take a straightening comb and straighten our hair. I loved going to see grandma, because we knew we would be treated well, but those days when my stepdad was in one of those moods and they had promised to take us to see her and they didn't; we would be so hurt. I remember praying to God to help us and He did. That is when my grandmother Marie adopted us. She came to Florence, SC with my biological father brother, Uncle Lenny, who was a big help to my grandmother. Uncle Lenny is a minister and singer. I really thank God for him, because he made sure my grandmother had whatever she needed to take care of us. When we had doctor visits, dentist appointments, birthdays, Christmas, whenever she needed help with anything he was right there. He was like the father I never had, and for that reason alone I will always be thankful and love my Uncle Lenny. My grandmother eventually was the guardian of all five of us. My grandmother and Uncle Lenny went all the way to Georgia to get my baby sister from DSS. Out of my mother five children, three belonged to my stepdad; me and my sister that was 2 years younger than me had different fathers. I was about seven, Shawna was five, John was three, and CoCo was about one or two. At that time, my grandmother had to be about 50 years old, and had already raised 10 children of her own by herself. We grew up in a small town called Bingham. Bingham was out in the woods, and the only thing we could see was trees and deers. My grandmother also was a Christian woman, who devoted her life to serving God and raising my siblings and me. She brought us up in church. Seem as if we went to church every night; I got tired of church. I know that is horrible to say, but I used to tell my grandmother that when I got older and could make my own decisions, I was going to church when I got ready. I did not really mean that but as a child we say things that we do not really mean. My grandmother used to tell us the only places we could go is school, church, and back home. We could not stay with anybody not even relatives that much. We could not do anything that children our ages did. People used to ask my grandmother can Lucy stay with us; her answer would be "No, not this time." I used to think to myself when would be the time. I used to get so mad with her, but I know now that she was only looking out or my best interest. Grandma taught me how to cook and clean a house. Everything I know about cooking, I learned from her, and I knew she was an excellent cook, because everybody in the neighborhood knew her for cooking and keeping a clean house. As a child, some things happened to me that I could not tell anyone. I was afraid that if I did, someone would think I was lying. Therefore, I did as Mary out the Holy Bible did and ponded everything in my heart. I grew up with a lot of hurt, anger, and regret deep inside me. I blamed my mother and father for not being present in my life to show and tell me the right directions, but mainly I blamed myself for all the bad people that hurt me. It was wrong, but I did not know who to confide in so I took it to the one person I knew would never betray me: Jesus. He taught me to love those who spitefully used and abused me, and cast in the sea of forgiveness, but to never forget. What was about to start happening to me, I would never wish on my worst enemy. Something that makes you jump in your sleep, restless at night, and lose trust in those you thought you should/could trust. How dare someone take a child's trust and expect them to act or be the same!

# CHAPTER 2

## *Someone Please Help Me: Reaching out Silently*

Growing up in our family, we were always told to keep things to ourselves. More like see nothing; say nothing whether you did or did not; you still were advised not to say anything. I thought at age twelve that I was to keep everything, as the older folks would say, "hush hush." Therefore, I did. My grandmother and her sisters were very big on keeping things a secret. The type family we have is the kind that pretends to be close, but it is strange how that closeness is hidden. As a child, I always felt very isolated. I did not have a mother or father there to help me. Therefore, things began to happen to me that I could not understand. I have a cousin who is a very big liar. He lies about any and everything. If you were to ask him, what today is and it could be Tuesday, but he would swear up and down it was Wednesday. He lies for no reason at all. This cousin got so good at lying, he would pretend. I never really felt comfortable around him, because the Holy Bible says that if you lie, you will steal, and if you will steal you will kill. I never knew until this day why he bothered me. This cousin was my grandmother's great great nephew. He would come to our house and drink liquor and beer with my uncles and other male cousins, and when it was time to go home, he would pretend to be so intoxicated that he would pass out on our couch in the living room. I will never forget the night he came into my room. It was dark in the whole house especially in my room, and he was black himself. Now in my room, me and my other two sisters slept in the same bed. He would reach all the way to where I was and start fondling me. I did not know what to do. I did not know whether to scream, cry, wake my sisters, or just lay there. Therefore, I did what any other scared child would do; all the above. This molestation lasted about a year or so because our trailer burnt down and we had to go stay with one of my aunts and her four children. I felt a relief, but I did not know that relief would turn back into reality. In the beginning, I was happy about living with my aunt because she cooked like grandma, and made sure we had clean clothes. Most of all she spent time with me. She was like the mother I grew up longing for. Aunt Val was my mother's sister. She is about two years older than my mother is though. I was now around 13 or 14 years old. Aunt Val had a daughter that was two years younger than I was, but we got along so well. We played, laughed, joked, and teased about everything together. She was like another sister. Her name was Pearl. She had a story to tell too, but no one ever listened. I took in everything not knowing the same thing that was happening to me before would eventually happen to me again. Aunt Val had three children by this guy, who I grew to hate passionately. I know I should not have hated anyone, but people make you hate them. As I write this, I'm getting sick to my stomach just even remembering anything about him, and I try to understand why some older people prey on innocent children or helpless people but I can't grasp the concept. The fear of someone invading your space or body is something you cannot ever get over. I remember one night my aunt went out to a nearby club and she left us home with him. I was so frightened that I did not know what to do. I went to sleep praying that God would protect us all that night. He did not begin molesting me until about three months after we moved in with my aunt. I was about 14 years old now and my figure was starting to show. The first time he touched me, he came into the room so quite. All the girls slept in the same bed, but a predator always knows who or what to do. The room was dark so I could never see anything, but the fear always let me know that he was nearby or coming. He would first rub my legs. I would try to cough or do something thinking he would get scared and leave, but he never did until he was done. Seem like he would take spit from his mouth, put it on his fingers, and touch me in my private area. As a child, I did not understand what he was doing, but now that I am older, I know that he was trying to make my vagina feel wet so he could "get off." This went on for about three to four months while we were at my aunt's house. I wanted to tell someone especially my aunt, but I did not know how to tell her. Therefore, I came up with a plan. I told my sister, who was two years younger than me, to go tell our aunt that he tried to touch her, and see what she would say. As I thought, she got mad and told my sister to stop lying. I knew right then she would not believe me either, but what I could not understand is why? From that day forward, I never told another person. I wanted to tell my cousin Pearl because we were so close, but I figure some things are better left untold. I felt so bad for Pearl, because I knew I would be going back home and she might would have been his next victim. We stayed with my aunt for about six or seven months, and then we went back home because my grandma had a new trailer after the old one burnt. I was happy to be going back home, but sad in a sense. I knew that my cousin would miss me. I wanted her to come live with us if not for good then on the weekends. Therefore, I asked grandma if she could come and she said on the weekend. Pearl and I was so happy. I am now fifteen years. I am getting older, and I am curious to why all my siblings know their biological father and I do not. What really made me curious was the fact that at school we had to do a family tree. I told my teacher I could not do this because I did not have a father. My teacher then replied to me that this would be an excellent way to find out who my father was. I went home and showed my grandmother my project and I asked her who my father was. She replied to me, who did your mother tell you he was? Now that's the thing, my mother always said a guy named Carl Miles was my father and that he lived in New York City, but that's all I knew about this Carl Miles. I knew there probably was little truth to this story, but how was I to find out who my biological father was. I was just a child, and my family always kept things so secretive. I went on and did my family tree with my mother and stepdad history. There was still a void that no one could fill until I knew who he was, and I was not going to stop until I got the truth. So, I went to the one person that I knew had to tell me the truth; my biological mother. I was not taking I do not know for an answer. I grew up not knowing, and was about to turn sixteen I wanted, needed, and deserved to know. Not knowing that what I was about to learn would change my life for good and add more heartache to my life.

# CHAPTER 3

## *The Family Secret that Got Out/Cousins*

I am now approaching my sixteenth birthday and after growing up without a mother or father in my life, I thought I deserved to know who was my biological father. I was happy with my grandma, because of her and God made me the person I am today. My grandma was my backbone, and she taught me about life the best way she knew how. I asked God to give me the strength to take what life hands to me. My mother was living in Georgia at this time. I wrote her a letter expressing how I was feeling, and wanted to know whom my father was. She called me when she received the letter and she told me that she was not going to write back because she wanted to talk to me face to face. She came home a week after my sixteenth birthday, and we had that talk that until this day I dreaded. She told me the most disturbing news that I had ever heard. She told me that my biological father was my cousin. At that moment, I was numb and heartless. I felt nothing for my mother or father. I hated them both. She asked me what was I feeling or what I had to say. I told her that I had nothing to say. She told me that he had raped her and that is how she got pregnant with me. She said that he was about fifteen years older than she was and she did not know better, but I did. Other relatives including my biological father said that they acted as if they were boyfriend and girlfriend, and that it was not rape meaning it was consensual. I was confused, broken, and distressed. How could this be? My mother and father were first cousins; two sisters children. Normally children born to close relatives like that would be born mentally challenged, have birth defects, and some do not even live. Therefore, I realized that God put me here for a reason. I know this is very confusing, but think how this made me feel; sick and uneasy. I buried this too in my heart for so long. Now, my cousins by my father are my sisters and brothers. One of my sisters/cousin, we grew up tight. She would always ask her mother, which was my stepmother and cousin, if I could stay with them. My grandma would say no most of the time. I do not know if my grandma knew who my father was, but she always told me she did not so I believed her because she never lied to me before. I felt like she must have known something, because she never wanted me around my father children. I do not know if she saw the resemblance between me and my father's children and my father. Everyone even my father's wife knew it, because I have that gap between my teeth like him, and those big eyes like his people. I remember growing up not knowing any of this, I went to his house and me and his baby girl was outside running around playing, and I heard her call him daddy. Therefore, not thinking more into it, I called him daddy too, because children sometimes notice what other children says. He stopped me and grabbed me by my arm and asked me what did I call him, and he told me not to ever call him daddy, because he was not my daddy. I ran back next door to his mother house crying. That hurt me to my heart because I did not mean anything by calling him daddy, but I guess the guilt inside him hurt. So, one day me and his baby girl was riding the school bus home together, and she told me that somebody told her that we looked alike and that we could go for twins. I started laughing and she said that her oldest brother told her one time that I was their sister too. I thought about it for a minute, and said yeah my mother told me that too. What I told her that for? She went and told her mother, and it was a big mess. Her mother left my father for a month or so trying to get the truth out of him, but he kept denying me. One of my grandmother's sisters who were close to my daddy's wife told me that I was wrong for opening my mouth and telling my cousin that. She also, told me that if my dad and his wife were to split up, I would be the cause of it. This hurt my feelings very deep, because all my life I've been lied to and hurt, and when I say one thing about what was told to me, I get chewed out. I cried and asked God to help me through this time, and I would not say anything else about anything that happens in my life. My stepmother loved me as if I was her real daughter. She never made me feel bad about me being her husband's child. She always said that she knew I was his because out of any of his children, and he has ten children, I looked so much like him. She said what had hurt her the most was that he never told her the truth about me. I loved my stepmother because she accepted me and never made me feel like some other family members made me feel. As if, it was my fault and like I was asked to be born. My stepmother died my senior year in high school, and until this day, I miss her smiling face, because she loved me in spite of the situation. I have learned the Serenity Prayer to accept the things I cannot change, change the things I can, and ask God to give me strength to know the difference. High school days helped me pass the time away and I tried to learn all I could so I could apply it to my life. You live and you learn!

# CHAPTER 4

## High School Years and Graduation

I had attended Latta High School and graduated in 2004 with a Business Diploma. I was a very smart student. I really loved this school system because of the teachers. At this school, if someone did not learn anything it was because they turned a deaf ear to what they were being taught. Everything I know up until this point in my life, I would have to give credit to Latta High and my teachers that encouraged me throughout my high school years. I do not want to start naming names because I am afraid that I would forget someone, but there are some that stood out the most with me. I was somewhat like popular in school and mostly everyone knew me. I have had friends that I have kept dear through my adult years. Some of my good friends were Kim Moultrie, Tezra Palmer, Jill Coleman, Siara Grice, Brandon Lane, Brandon Lester, Emery Davis, Ethan Sansbury, Courtney Page, Sonesu McClellan, and Melinda Wheeler; these people I may have had falling out with, but we remain friends. I do have two best friends: Tramaine Spears and LaToya Eaddy; now these are like my sisters. We always had been close since elementary school.

They were popular in school, and we sometimes competed in things against one another, but wc did not fall out. Like for instance, our senior year 2004, we all ran for Miss LHS. Neither of us got mad with one another, but we did say that either way we would be happy with whoever got it because we loved each other. LaToya won Miss LHS. Tramaine and I were still happy. I love these girls because no matter what we went through, we always remained friends. LaToya and I used to stay mad with one another, but we always seem to get back close. I think it was more or less we were all so close, but we were afraid of one getting closer with the next one. Instead of us understanding either way, we all were best friends. Even up until this point, we are best friends, and we are there when one needs the other. I love you both Toy and Maine. You all do not know how important you were in my life growing up. I cherish our friendship forever because I knew my life was chaotic growing up and you all never knew because seeing the way you all never judged me let me know that there was hope for me. Thank you girls so much and I love you both will all my heart. High school years went by so fast that we did not keep up with the days or years. I took all college preparatory classes. Some classes were easier for me than others. Whereas Chemistry was hard for me, but the teacher Mrs. KC made it fun. She tried her best to teach and make Chemistry interesting, but when I do not understand something then it is difficult to make me understand. There was a secretary at LHS, Ms. Grissett. I loved her, but none of the other students did because they said she was too noisy, but she never bothered me. She always gave me encouraging words and smile. I have had other teachers that I love up until this day: Mr. Goodwin, Mrs. Manning, Mrs. Herndon, and Mrs. Rogers. Now between my keyboarding teachers, I am tough as an iron pipe on a computer thanks to those two teachers. I can type 60+ wpm; I know the functioning of a computer, all the different types of programs, etc. I love typing thanks to them, and I know so much about computers, computer software, and computer programming thanks to them. Now there is a teacher in particular that I have to take time out to thank; Mrs. Myra Elvington. She was my English and Grammar teacher. This woman to me was a grammar queen; she knew everything there was to know about speaking etiquette, putting your verbs, nouns, and pronouns where they go in sentences or speaking in general. I grew to love this woman. It broke my heart that my sophomore or junior year she was going to leave our school. Therefore, our class of 2004 wanted to show our gratitude to her, we had a program for her in the gymnasium to show and tell her how much she had done for us. The class voted me to give the speech. As I begin to write up what to say to her, I asked God to guide me in what to say to let her know that she inspired my life in so many ways. As I was up to read what the Lord gave me to say, I began to cry knowing that she was the one teacher that opened my eyes to what I loved to do which is writing. I brought back to her remembrance that before anyone can finish high school, it was a test you have to take called the Exit Exam; she gave us one item in particular that helped me to stay awake during the exam: a peppermint. I let her know that just like that, peppermint saved me on the exam, she saved me and taught me about having a passion for writing, and until this day, I love her so dearly. Wherever you are Mrs. Elvington, you are one of my inspirations, because you opened my eyes to my first love; writing. Thank you so very much. Now, there were good and bad moments in high school that I will cherish forever in my heart. One would be when I lost my virginity.

I want speak much on this topic, but if it was one moment that I regretted in high school, it would be that day before my 18th birthday. The guy was not any good, but as young and dumb females we sometimes to fall for the guys that do not respect us. This thing with this guy lasted for about two years until I got up enough nerve to stop him from making a fool out of me. I had feelings for him because he took my virginity, and at the same time he grew on me as a good friend. I want say his name but he knows who he is and until this day, only a few people know about him. That is my little secret and that is how I will keep it. I went to both my junior and senior prom. I enjoyed them both. Now I am approaching my senior year in high school. This was a sad year for me even though at the end of every school year I would cry. I do not know until this day why I would be the only one crying, but my senior year was different I knew why I was crying. I knew that everyone would be going his or her separate ways and some good friends I would probably never see again. It was like a bittersweet moment. Our senior year was fun though. I finally tried out for track and field. I made the team. I was so excited because some of my friends that have been running since our freshman year were on the team. I did place in some the events, which allowed me to go to State and Lower State Championship. I really enjoyed my senior year. It went by so fast though. Graduation was in May of 2004, a day I will cherish and never forget. I remember practicing the day before graduation, and the principal calling out the names of our classmates. Everyone was laughing because we did not know some of our classmate's whole names. It was too funny to us; we would joke about it after the fact. High school days were what they were. They were to prepare us for our future as young adults. Some took advantage of what we learned at LHS and furthered their careers, and some went on to start a family. Thanks to the staff at Latta High School for all you all have done to teach me what I know today. It will be forever embedded in my mind and heart. As my Grandmother would always say "education will take you as far as you want to go if you apply yourself, and sky is the limit." So, college here I come!

# CHAPTER 5

## *Learning to Live/College Life*

I was one of the people in high school that some people would have said was "college material." I would have had to disagree not because I was not smart or did not have the grades, but I was not a people person. Some would say I am just like my grandmother, because she stayed to herself. I mean people grow to love me when they meet and get to know me, but I always was so insecure. I thought people would judge me on my outward appearance before getting to know the real Alicia. My grandmother always used to say that sky is the limit now days for an education; therefore, I knew she wanted me to go to college. I wanted to sit out the year after I graduated because I thought I was in love. This guy was originally from New Jersey. We had been going out for about two years. He was tall, light complexion, muscular built, and very supportive of me. I thought he would have been my husband. To make it short and nice, he went back to NJ to visit his mother and siblings. He stayed up there for about three months and called me one day; a day I will never forget. He told me that he was not coming back down South and for me to take care of myself. When he told me this on the phone, I was very devastated and hurt. I went walking to Aunt Val's house crying so hard I did not see a long distance truck that liked to hit me. I did not know what to feel. I finally got over this major first love. After about a month or two, his cousin called and told me that he was in like a mental hospital because someone had laced his marijuana. This then really took a toll on me. I wanted to see him, hold him, and just let him know that I was there, but everyone told me it would be no use because it had messed up his brain. He now considered schizophrenic. After all, of this, I decided to go to college because there was not anything in Bingham for me to do. In high school I had to take either the ACT or SAT; I took the ACT and scored good. I applied North Carolina A & T, Fayetteville State University, and Coastal Carolina. I was accepted to two of the three, but when I went to tour the schools, I did not feel comfortable. I knew a couple of people who went to South Carolina State University in Orangeburg, SC, and they told me that it was a good school. I did not want to go to State because some said it was considered a "party" school, but I know now that was not true. I applied to SC State and within a week time, I was accepted. My grandmother was so excited for me. She told me the day I was leaving that I was leaving as one and that I had better come back as one. She was trying to tell me that I better not get a baby while I was away at college. When I got in the car to leave, I could see that my grandma was sad, but pleased. That is all I wanted to do was to make her proud, because she made me proud of just being a good mother to me and my siblings. It is now 2005, and I was starting for the fall semester majoring in Elementary Education. I stayed in this field of study for most of my freshman year and my sophomore year; I changed my major to Family and Consumer Science Business. This was more up my alley, because it had a variety of fields I could go into with just this one degree. I was lucky to have a roommate whose mother was a librarian at the college. They were so nice to me. They helped me the first day of registration, showed me where I needed to go, and what to do. My roommate and I grew to be very close. She was from Summerville, SC. She was the first person that introduced me to college drugs. Let me go head and say "marijuana." No other drugs did we do. When I say this girl could smoke; she smoked more than a chimney. She would wake up smoking, go to bed smoking, and if she could smoke in her dreams, I believe she would have. I remember when I first smoked with her and our other friends, I was something crazy. I laughed when there was nothing funny, laughed whenever anybody said anything; everything was so funny. From that night on, we smoked. She taught me the basics to smoking. She told me that whenever I brought my first bag of weed, and rolled my first blunt, I would "officially" be considered a smoker. I did all this, and just knew I was bad to the bones. For the first time in my life, I felt like I fitted in. I was accepted for whom I was, and for that reason, alone I continued to smoke with her. We were like two peas in a pot wherever you saw her you saw me and vice versa. She became one of my best friends in college. We had our difficulties especially when I came to smoking sometimes. I had not got as good as she had with smoking like in the morning times. One cold winter morning she got up and wanted to go outside with her to smoke, and I told her no she got mad and wanted to talk trash. I then called her a "pot head." I did not know that people get so offended by that word. I later apologized to her because she started crying saying that I hurt her feelings. We did slow up on the smoking though. We tried to enjoy the rest of our college years together because she only had one more year and I was just getting there. My sophomore year which would have been her junior/senior year, she moved into the athletic apartments because she had made the cheerleader squad, and I didn't want to get to know any other roommate I moved off campus with a lady I met in summer school. I met Natasha and her daughter my freshman year of summer school. We were taking Biology together. We hit it off real well; she was like an older sister. We were so acquainted that I met her family and she met some of mine. When we would get our refund checks from State, we would go to Columbia, SC and shop until we dropped literally. That is what we liked to do when we were not having guys chase us. Natasha is about 31 years old now. She taught me a lot in the two years I was at State. We still keep in touch until this day. State is a good HBCU (Historically Black College University). I did learn while I was there. When people say now days that State is a party school, I simply correct them and let them know that State is what you make it. The years I was there, I went out to a club twice. I did what I did while I was there, but it only was a learning experience. Sometimes we as young adults, think we are ready to make a change that we think will be for the best, but it turns out to be a change for the worst. We learn that people and situations change.

# CHAPTER 6

## *The Charge to Keep I Have*

Latta is just like Bingham; small. No matter where I go, I always will remember where I came from. Sometimes people move to different places to start over or start a better life, but there is one thing that I have learned to do in life and that is to remember. We can sometimes try to forget but it is hard, because it is, where you come from that will get you to where you are going. My grandma raised me to mind my own business, speak when spoken to, and see nothing say nothing. She said that this would get you far in life. I am not the type of person to cause problems. I do just as my grandma taught me to do. What I realized by doing this that people think that you are afraid of them and that you want stand up for what you know is right. My sophomore year at State, I ran into a girl that graduated from my high school a year before I did. She told me that she had a house off campus and she was looking for roommates. Now in high school this girl was quite, was a nobody (meaning she could have died and nobody would have noticed), she was not that well known and not too popular. She moved to Orangeburg to go to State after she graduated from high school. This was my first time seeing her since 2003. She looked about the same dark skin, pimples, somewhat big boned, and no shape. The only difference was that she had joined a sorority (AKA), which made her feel popular and like she was somebody now. That is what college will do the nobody's of the world. To make a long story short, I end up moving in with her. Two other girls live there too. One was from Mullins, SC and the other one was from Charleston, SC. The first day that I moved in the house with them, I should have known it was going to be problems. Soon as I got there, she started talking about the girl from Mullins. I am thinking okay this girl has been here with you before I got here and as soon as I come, you want to talk about her to me; I could imagine what you would be saying about me. I did not participate in her small talk; I guess that is one reason we hit it off wrong. Then it was a guy that my niece used to date came over to the house to see me. He brought along some of his friends so we can could smoke and chill. She gets mad and when they left, she asked me was I sleeping with him. I told her that my niece to date him and that is how I knew him. She then replied that she was just asking because two people living in the same house cannot be sleeping with the same guy. This was my first day I moved in the house. I should have listened to my instincts and moved back out. I stayed there for about six months. The girl from Mullins was nice. She had a boyfriend that she introduced me to. He was sexy to me, but I never told her that. Being that it was an alliance in our house, my roommate from Mullins and her boyfriend would visit me in my room and vice versa. When she was in class, he would stop by, and when she was not in class, he would stop by. Therefore, the roommate that kept everything going makes up a lie to my other roommate telling her that I was sleeping with her boyfriend when she would leave to go to class. I was furious about this and confronted my roommate. We end up fussing. She would wake up early in the morning slamming the bathroom doors and kitchen cabinets just to make me upset. Finally, one night I got tired of playing these kitty games with her, my niece ex-boyfriend and my roommate from on campus came to get me. My roommate from hell told him he was not welcomed at "her" house even though all of us split the bills equally. At this time, I was upset and I went to ask her why she told him that because he was my company and she had no right to turn him around at the door. We end up fighting that night. It was the end of the semester and finals were going on. We had to go to a court hearing for her to evict me out the house. She ends up winning the case because her and her mother came to the hearing lying. I went along with it and did not try to contest anything. I had to spend my money and stay in a hotel room for three days so I could finish my finals. Until this day this girl acts like she does not like me, but I let that go a long time of go. I guess when you whip someone's behind that well they should not have anything to say to the other person. She now has two children and people tell me that her boyfriend beats on her. I feel sorry for her if this is true because no female should have a man putting his hands on them, but at the same time the type person she was she probably don't leave the guy any other choice. I am not condoning violence in any way and if it means anything, I forgave her and wish her the best in life. It was December, the semester was over, and I had to go back to Latta and face other haters. I was now talking to a guy who was cousins to one of good high school friends. This guy and I hit it off real good. We had been talking now about a year, but he was incarcerated about six months into our relationship. I started to care for this guy. I always seem to fall for guys that are not about anything maybe because I thought I could change them in some type of way. This guy had this girl pregnant before we got together. This girl was known for sleeping around town with everyone; so, it could have been anyone's baby. I dealt with this because it was before my time. When she had the baby that is when all the problems began. I would go out to a little club in Latta. She would see me and she would want to start picking. She would waste her drink on me, try to walk in the door of the club the same time I did, bump me, etc. I never would say anything because I knew most of the time she was either drunk or high off cocaine. There was a night in particular; I could not 'let any other picking continue to go on. It was the night I went out with my now ex-boyfriend's family. The baby mama goes so jealous that she started the same things she would normally do. She stomped on my new timberland boots inside the club and I did not do anything. After the club, is when everything got heated. She called herself going to the car, getting her coat, and trying to put it on. She took the sleeve of the coat and swapped me across my face and at this time, I could not take any more picking. We ended up fighting and I cut her up. She took out a warrant on me for assault and battery with attempt to kill. I did not try to kill her, but I just wanted to remind her the next time she wanted to pick, for her to look at what she would get. We ended up going to court. She ended up dropping the warrant because she was already going to court for lynching. I was so happy because I did not do anything wrong except protect myself. I don't' bother anyone unless they are trying to harm me, and when I feel like someone is out to harm me then like anyone, I have to protect myself.

I love my life and freedom, and for someone to think they can take either of them from then they must be God. When the Lord helped me to get out of both situations, I did not look back. I just went back to Orangeburg to visit in 2009. I try to learn from life lessons. As my deceased Uncle John loved to sing about "it was a charge to keep I have, but to glorify God above." I knew that God would see me out of any difficult situations. I knew that there was not anything too hard for God. I learned like in the Holy Bible days when the Lord delivered a woman from her sins; Jesus told her to go in peace and sin no more, and that is what I have attempted to do. When I pray, I always ask God to lead me in the directions that He would have me go in and lead me not into temptations. The Lord allows His children to be tested, and the devil can only do what God allows him to do. I know if God take s me to it, He will bring me through it.

# CHAPTER 7

## The Same Sex Relationship

When life seems unbearable, then the unwanted happens; it gets even more unbearable. I found myself in a place that I never dreamed I would ever be. A place that God was not pleased with and a lifestyle that He frowned upon; I found myself in the same sex relationship. Some would question what made me turn this way, but in my heart and mind, I felt like it was something I had to endure in order for God to make my faith in Him stronger. We go through things in life that God does not condone, but He allows us to experience it to help others. Some would say how did this happen? I cannot say that I came on to her or she came on to me; it was just something that happened. I met AJ through my aunt that I went to live with after I came home from college. She appeared to me not as a woman but as a man. She talked, walked, and even dressed like a man. There was nothing feminine about her except she had two children. She would come to my aunt house every day after she would get off work. I would say some things to her, but never would I make eye contact because I felt that people like that could easily persuade anyone. As time went by, she and her girlfriend at the time was going through some problems, and she would come and talk about them to me. I would listen and give her advice on what I would do if it were I in that predicament. We then exchanged cell phone numbers and that is where it all began. We would text each other in the morning, after she would get off work, and at night before we went to sleep. It became an everyday thing, and that is where the feelings came in. We got so close that she would sometime spend the night at my aunt's house with me. Then one night we were lying on the floor talking and she was telling me what it was like to be with a woman, because I was asking her what she could do for a woman that a man could not. I was telling her that a woman could not satisfy me as if a man could. She just sat there and laughed. She then told me that her tongue could unlatch. I asked her what does that mean. She then took one of her Newport 100's cigarettes and placed it on the floor in front of me; she told me that her tongue was that long. I did not ask any more questions and we went to sleep. Time went by and we got closer but I did not see her as female. Seem like in my mind I saw her as a female but in my heart, I wanted her to be a man so bad. I knew it was wrong, but I was starting to have real feelings for her. Nobody could tell any different; everyone was trying to figure out whether we were in a relationship, but at this particular time, we were not. It was now about January or February 2007 court had turned out in my favor and I was happy and wanted to celebrate. She asked me to go to a room with her. She said that she would pay for the room and if I did not trust her like that, she would buy a room for my cousin Bonnie and whomever she wanted to take with her. I told her no at first, but then I changed my mind. This is when everything happened and I could not turn back then. I want go into detail about what happened but it changed my view on same sex relationships. From that night forward, we made it official that we were in a relationship. In the beginning, she treated me better than some guys I had previously been in a relationship with. She gave me whatever I wanted. She brought me 10 karate cluster rings for all ten of my fingers, XO's necklaces, shoes, clothes, money and mostly anything I asked for she would try to get it for me. That made me fall in love with her even more. At this point and time, we were not staying together; I was still living with my aunt and AJ was at her own house. Finally, she asked me to move in with her. I knew everything would change between us, because like every other relationships when people began to be around their mate for a long period of time, the relationship changes because you began to see the person for whom they really are. At first when I moved in everything was good. We got along so well even down to her children. At the time, AJ's oldest daughter Kami was about sixteen and the baby girl Naomi, whom I bonded with so well was ten. Now AJ's oldest daughter is my cousin by her father, but I did not know who her father was until I moved in with them. Kami and I did not always see eye to eye on things because our attitudes were so much alike. I do not know if she felt like I was trying to take her place in the household of taking care of her little sister or what it was. I had taken Naomi under my wings because I felt a connection with her. She was like I was growing up; meaning she kept all her feelings bottle up inside and seemed to always be angry. I knew where she was coming from because really she never had time with her mother or father. AJ always had girlfriends that she always seemed to spend time with, and Naomi sensed that she never had time for her. She felt neglected. Then her father was married to someone else and taking care of her and children. Naomi just felt neglected on every hand, and that is why I felt like she needed me to help her. I tried to guide her in the right directions telling her difference between right and wrong. She would get attitudes with me, but we got that understanding now because she knew that I genuinely loved and cared for her and out of AJ's past girlfriends I took up time with her. Until this day, we still have that bond. As time progressed in the household, some days where better than others were, because I started watching AJ's habits. I began to see how she would abuse pain medication, beer, and cigarettes. Every day she would take Percocet pills, drink about a six-pack of beer, and smoke a pack of the 100's Newport until she got high and went to sleep. This worried me and I began to say something to her about it. She would then tell me that she had been doing this for a long time and if something were going to happen to her, it would have been happened. I told her on several occasions that I would leave her if she did not quit. She would sometimes get her gun and say that she would kill herself if I left her because she had nothing to live for. One time she locked herself in the bathroom and cut her arm with a knife, and sometimes she would act as if she was having a seizure just for me to stay. I mean I never seen anyone do things that she did to keep me there with her. Therefore, I began to analyze things. People was just looking at the small picture seeing two females together, but I realize that it was a greater need for me to be with her. She was about 20 years older than I was, but age did not matter because when someone is in need it does not matter who is older. I began to ask her to tell me what her childhood was like. She immediately began to cry. She confide in me. I want go into her childhood, but I always wondered why we connected. People did not understand her but this is what turned her from men. Many people look at people that are in the same sex relationships as to be gross or look down on them instead of getting to know what caused them to be this way. Therefore, I would pray every night before going to bed, and the would just lay there and listen. Things got a little better between us, but it was not any sexual things going on as if it was in the beginning. We had now been together about a year and a half. At this time, I began to have a major problem in my life, my grandmother, Marie, that had raised me from a child up, is now sick and in the hospital. It was like February or March 2008, and my birthday had come around. I do not know what I started feeling. I began to pray even more now. The Lord has been good to me in spite of the situations. He blessed me with a job at Spring Branch Treatment Center, which is a drug and alcohol social detox facility, and my own apartment. At this time, I was feeling alone and hurt, but at the same time, I was trying to be strong for everyone. I was neglecting my feelings and dwelling on asking the Lord to help my grandma get better. AJ was still AJ. She was doing the same things that I told her I did not like her doing. She was hurting herself and could not see it. We were coming up on our two-year anniversary, but I ready to be out of this lifestyle. I tried to help her, but what I did not understand that if someone is not willing to help himself or herself then it would not work. I got tired of looking out for her well-being that I began to feel my spiritual life go down and I was bringing myself down in the end. I prayed that last prayer and asked God with sincerity to remove me out the current situation I was in. I had prayed the same prayer before, but this time He knew I had enough. I ended up moving in my own apartment and staring a new life on my own. I just sometimes wished my grandmother had been here to see me now. She did not like me being with a woman, but she never made her feel or me unwelcome. The only thing she said was that I know I was not raised like that. As I stated previously, I knew all of that was true, but I knew God would forgive me and not to go back. Until this day AJ and I communicate from time to time, but we both got the understanding that she and I could never be again. This was just a learning part in my life and I know that God is pleased in my decisions I have made up until this point. He knew when I was going to be in this relationship with this woman and when I was going to let it go. I have a picture my house that AJ brought me and it says that God would not take you to things if He were not going to bring you through it. I believe this, and I can truly say that it was God that brought me through this. I found out through this point in my life that the people that were for me. People talked about me, but the most hurtful thing was that it was mainly family and so-called friends. There were some of both that stuck by me through it all, and for those and you know who you are; thank you and those who talked about us thank you all also. What people did not know is that God never once took His hands off me. He loved me in spite of what I did. He says in the Holy Bible, "He without sin; cast the first stone," and there is no sin greater than the next, but what He did tell me to go in peace and sin no more. I love Jesus because He is so gracious and merciful. He could have wiped us both off the face of the earth as He did back in the biblical days, but He knew He had a greater purpose and plan for my life. What the devil means for bad, God mean it for my Good! You should always cherish the important people in your life while they are living, because the Holy Bible says that man born of a woman must surely die.

# CHAPTER 8

## The Death of Someone Special

Some people may say that we are put on this earth for a season, and there are those would argue different. I am one of those people that would argue different, because I thought my grandmother would never leave me. She was strong as a rock. I mean my grandma would turn homemade cornbread with her bare hands instead of with the spatula, she would plunder in junk so hard her back would be hurting and she still would be plundering, and most of all she raised fifteen children in all her ten children and myself and four other siblings. In February 2009, I got a phone call from my aunt stating that my grandmother was being rushed to the ER because she could not breathe. I jumped in my car coming from Latta, SC doing eighty miles all the way to Dillon, SC not caring whether a police would stop me, because I knew she really had to be sick in order for her to be going to the ER. Let me first explain why I say this. As I stated earlier in another chapter that my grandma raised me since I was about six years old and I am currently 25 years old and I never heard talk or saw my grandma go to a doctor. If anything she would tell us to go, but she would not dare go herself. My aunt, which is my grandma's baby girl, she is about thirty-five years old and that was the last time my grandma saw a doctor was when she had her. So, this night that she was being rushed to the ER, I knew she had to be very sick. I believe I beat the rescue squad to the hospital and they were coming from Bingham. When I saw my grandma laying up there on that stretcher, I could not do anything except cry. They had an oxygen mask around her mouth and nose, and the paramedic was squeezing it trying to help her breathe. I was so hurt because I never saw my grandma sick before. I wanted to help her and I could not. I wanted to trade places with her, because that was my rock laying up there so helpless. She could not talk, she could not do anything not even breath for herself. That made me feel so bad; felt like a part of me had died that night even though she was still alive, I knew right then that she would never be the same. When they got her in the back to be seen by the doctor, everything was going wrong and because she had not seen a doctor in about thirty years, she did not know she was a diabetic. Her sugar was about 500 or more, her blood pressure was up, she had a giardia on her neck the size of a grapefruit, and that was what was cutting off her windpipe circulation. So, she was very sick, but God kept her seventy years without even knowing she was sick. I know that everyone on this earths days are numbered because the Holy Bible tells me, but I never thought that it would be like this and that soon. I know she lived passed the days that God promised man three scores and ten, which is seventy years, but I miss her so much. She did live months after this happened. She went to McLeod in Florence, SC and the doctors over there said that really there was nothing they could do for her. She had a slight heart attack; they did remove the giardia off her neck, her kidneys and live had begun to shut down. Our family is a firm believer that God want put more on you than you can bear. My grandma end up coming home and my aunts and uncles took turn caring for her. This went on about four months. We just knew she was going to be here longer but the unthinkable happened. The day before she died, I tried my hardest to get out there to see her. I was actually going to spend the night, but when I got out there, I was too sick to stay. Let me tell you all how the Lord works in mysterious ways. I was trying to wait around for my cousin to come so I could do her hair to make some money for gas to go to Bingham, but seem like she was never coming. I told my aunt to tell her that I would be in the country whenever she came. I had no money, no gas but I knew some way I had to get out there to see my grandma, and that day was like no other I was persistent about getting out there. I got down the road about ten miles out, and guess what happens; I ran out of gas. There were people passing by, but God always have his children an angel. This black man came and he told me that he had a gas jug if I wanted him to go get me some gas. I told him that I did not have any cash on me and he left. I thought for sure I was stranded. I end up seeing him come back and he had me ten dollar's worth of gas. I got his name and number so that when I got his money I could call him. I got out there to the country to see my grandma and she was laying in the bed still so helpless, but this time it was different. She was groaning and moaning in a way that sounded as if she was in pain. Her sister was in the room with her, and I asked her why she was sounding like that. She replied she been like that all morning and night. I sat down beside my grandma to let her know that Lucy was there. I grabbed her hand, and I began to sing the song I sung for her when she was in the hospital. The words to the song goes a little like this: "Oh, grandma, I want you to know I love you, please forgive me for all the times I broke your heart, and every tear you cried for me to be closer to being free and I want to thank you and I thought you would like to know." When I sang this song for her, I could see her eyes water up and a tear would drop. I began to pray with her. I said Lord you said that you would not have your children suffering and I felt that my grandma was suffering and in pain. I said Lord if it is your will please let your will be done, and that instant I felt a relief that I never felt before came across me. That was my sign then that the Lord heard my cry and I believe in my heart that my grandmother had to be praying in her heart the same prayer. I kissed my grandma on the forehead and told her that I loved her. I then told my aunt that I had to go because I had to go to work. I was lying, but I could not tell her that this sick feeling had come across me and I had to leave quickly. I believe that if you live close to God, He will give you a sign when someone close to you is not doing well or if they are about to leave. I did not realize the sign until that next morning around four, my aunt, which is my grandma's oldest daughter called me crying hysterically. She told me "Ree gone Lucy." I could not do anything but drone the phone and cry. I was in disbelief, but what came to me was that I got there to her and thanks to that man. I do not remember his name but I want to thank him so much because he allowed God to use him to get me out there to see my grandma before she died. To this mystery angel, thank you. You do not know how much that meant to me; you are one of the reasons that I am sane. Thank you again. We went out there that night to the house. She was laying there as if she was at peace. I cried until I got sick. I knew the prayer I had prayed that day before, and God had to have heard my prayer. A part of me was happy because she would not have to suffer anymore, but there is that human side that is selfish and wanted to keep her here with me. Nobody really understood the way I felt for my grandma and she never really showed emotions but we knew she loved us and that is how I felt. The whole time she was sick, my aunts and uncles had to take care of her, and I spent a night at the hospital. I was too hurt. I know everybody especially her ten children were hurt, but my grandmother was more to me than a family member. She was my rock and my earthly angel. She is the reason besides God that I am where I am today. After all that I have been through in my 25 years of living, she kept me at peace. As long as I knew she was there, I knew I would be okay. She took care of me when nobody else cared to. She took my siblings and me in when she was sick herself but nobody knew. She was my precious jewel. On the obituary, my aunts and uncles let me write the poem for her from me. It was entitled "Precious Jewel." When I think of a jewel, I think of something so sacred that you would hate to lose, and if you were to lose that jewel, you would feel sad and lost. That is how I felt when my grandma died. I was in state of disbelief and I wanted to go in a hole and die. My heart had been torn out and my mind began to travel back down memory lane, but God kept me under His wing. He knew that my heart could not take any more pain; that is why He allowed me to go home that day before she died and not stay at her house. He knew that my heart could not take it and that is how I know that the Lord want put any more on us then we can bear. I am stronger now thanks to my grandma. She died September 21, 2008, but she will forever live in my heart. Grandma, I miss you so much. Words cannot even begin to describe the pain I felt when you died, but I am content with it now, because I said my goodbyes, and I treated you like my jewel that I will never lose. I love you grandma and you can rest in peace because I am okay now. You gave me the key to the doors, and all I have to do is unlock it. You never told me that you loved me, but I knew that you did because of the actions you showed me. Jesus said if you love me, you will keep my commandments. After everything I've been through, I had to learn how to love and trust again.

# CHAPTER 9

## *Life Lesson–Learning to Love Myself*

Some may say that it might be the feelings of unworthiness that we have carried with us our whole lives. Others may say that we learn to feel a certain way about ourselves by the way we are treated growing up. As for me, I had no self-esteem, I hated everything about myself, and I sometimes wished I was never born. I know this sounds horrible, but my life felt like a mistake. Everything that I have endured up until where I am now in life made me wish I was not ever born. I used to listen to some of my friends talk about their family and I would get jealous. I wished I had their lives sometimes. As a child, I never had a mother or father to show me love, but I did have my grandma but there is nothing like a biological mother and father love toward their child. There is always that void that no one no matter how hard they try to fill they could not. I used to long for that love from my parents so much that I began to be molested and I thought it was okay. I got older and that guilt of not telling anyone grew into hate towards me. In addition, when I would look in the mirror all I could see is the gap between my teeth that comes from my father, which made me, hate myself even more. I felt like that made me so ugly. This gap between my teeth prevented me from doing many things I wanted to do in high school. I wanted to cheer and play sports or run for things, but because my self-esteem was too low; I did nothing. Everything I endured in my life so far made me hate "me." As I got older, I began to have different boyfriends. I still had this unworthiness and since of not being pretty so I would second-guess the guys that would want to be in a relationship with me. They would tell me that they loved me or was falling in love with me, and I would do something to make them not love me. I did not know that my hate towards myself was rubbing off on them too. I began to sit down and think what I was doing wrong. I got back into church and began to read my bible. God said that everything that He made was good. I tried to find good things about myself. Therefore, I turned to the one thing that made me feel happy which was writing. I began to write poems for my relationships and my feelings about life in general. I began to feel better about myself, because I knew that writing was something I was good at. In life, I learned that you have to find your niche and mine was writing. I still was a little uncomfortable with myself, and I tried to change me, but that is one thing I have learned in order to love yourself you have to love everything about you and then work on the flaws. "If you long to be the sort of person who is caring and forgiving, you first have to start with yourself, and if you can forgive yourself for your shortcomings and imperfections, you can then love yourself." I read this in a magazine article one day at work. I knew this was speaking directly to me; so, I took the advice and began to pray to God to help me to love myself. I asked Him to help me forgive those people who had hurt me from my past to present, and then let me able to forgive myself.

I got into another relationship. This guy was different. He was tall, dark skin complexion, had neat dreads, he could dress from head to toe, had a job, no children, and his own car. I used to conversate with him when I was in high school and we went on a date to the movies and I ran back into him 2009 and we exchanged numbers. We hit if off real well for the first 2 months, but my loneliness and insecurities made me start pushing him away. He worked third shift on his job and he would get off work the next morning and sleep all day long but I did not believe him. I wanted him here with me, because when I was around him seem like I felt safe and secure. He would hold me all night long and make me feel like I was the only one that mattered. It was hard for me to trust men because of what happened to me growing up, but I felt good about him. The only thing I did not like about him was that he loved to go to the club every weekend. I knew this before we got together and he would have to want to change that. We began to get into arguments until he just said we are better off as friends. I cried to him many times telling him that I loved him even after we broke it off. I told him my life story one night when we were talking, and he replied to me something that I will never forget. He told me to love you first and that I did not know anything about love because I did not know how to love me first. Until this day, I thank him because he opened my eyes to something that was real. I cannot love anybody until I love myself. I did not realize what he was saying until I went home and really thought and prayed on it. The reason I could not love myself because I had not forgiven myself of the guilt I have grown up with all my life. I wanted to be love so bad by other people that I did not know how to love Alicia. This guy really got through to me. I felt like we were meant to be because I was always told that if it comes back to you then you are meant to be. It had been five years since I had seen him and when we had ran back into each other, I was trying to find a way to get out the relationship with the woman. I just knew he was the one, but he was the one who taught me my life lesson. I would like to thank you Jo for showing me how to love myself even though we are not together you will always hold a dear place in my heart because you opened my eyes to reality. Love is something that takes time and commitment. Jo would say we taking it one day at a time. I wanted to jump right into a relationship, but love does not work like that. Like for instance, love is like a flower that does not bloom overnight. That flower need sunlight, water, and tender love and care, and when it get all those things that gives it the nutrients it need to grow and bloom into a beautiful flower. Love works the same way. Learning to love was hard for me, but the Holy Bible taught me to love that who spitefully used me and that is what I have done. Now I have learned to love Alicia. Learning to love me was hard at first, but now I realize it was easy all along, because I did nothing wrong except learned how and when to love. I was hiding behind guilt and hatred that I could not see the wonderful things about myself. I love myself now and I owe it to those who has hurt and used me, those that said I would never amount to anything because of where I came from, but most of all those who laughed about my short coming and took me for granted. I am me, and I cannot and would not change that. All I can do is start living life the way God had intended for me to. I am happy with where I am in life now. I am working at a Drug and Alcohol Facility in I have been employed for two years, and I am working part time at Cititrends. I have my own apartment fully furnished and my car a 2003 Nissan Altima (black). I am attending college online at Capella University to finish my Bachelor's Degree in Business Administration. I am proud of my accomplishments because I thought I would never be happy. I am happy, single, and living and loving life. I am learning every day how to love me even more. Life is full of lies, but it is left up to you whether you let life lies keep you from loving you.

# CHAPTER 10

## *My Testimony*

Many are afraid to tell what he or she has been through in life. Some would say that it is not anybody's business, but I say different. I was brought up in church and was always taught that your testimony can help someone else. You never know someone could be going through the same thing you have or are going through, but if neither one of you will know if one don't take the initiative to say something first. I was at one time afraid of what people would say or think about me, but I do not care anymore. I care about the hurting people out there that can use some encouraging word and to let them know that God is able. People are going to criticize you if you are doing good or bad; so, why not start telling the truth. The things that I have overcome in my short 25 years of living, I pray that it can help someone come up out of their situations. Many people my age have not experienced anything and then there are some that have, but I took the step to help me began my healing process. I am speaking out and letting everyone know including my family because I was tired of holding these feelings of guilt inside when I am not the one who has done wrong. I did not ask to be brought into this world, but now that I am here, there is not anything anyone can do about it except learn to love me, as I have had to learn to do. No, I am not proud of where I come from, but God makes no mistake. There is purpose behind pain is what I tell myself. Many would say that God had no part in my mother and father sleeping together and they were first cousins, but my Bible tells me that God is omniscient meaning He is all knowing meaning He knew Alicia before Alicia knew herself. He said that He knows the strand of hairs on my head and a beautician does not even know that. God has a plan for each one of our lives including mine. He knew everything I would go through in life, because He knew that one day I would be able to withstand the trick of the devil and get up enough courage to take back what the devil thought he stole from me. All those negative things that happened to me in my life was only the trick of the enemy to try to keep my mouth close and keep me in bondage, but I spoke to that storm one day and it had to cease. Whitney Houston came back with a song that said, "I look to you." She said that she was not made to break; I like that. Everything I have been through, the average young person would have turned to drugs, prostitution, or worst self-murder, but I turned to the one person as Whitney said; I turned to God. I asked Him to give me my purpose in life and to help me get over the obstacles in life that sometimes keep me in one place. I do not want to be the victim anymore. I do not want to walk around with my head down not knowing which way to turn. I found a book in bag I got from a thrift store entitled "Making Peace with Your Past" written by H. Norman Wright, and I haven't read it yet but there were chapters that stood out to me as I was scanning through. Some were Excess Baggage-Where

Can You Put It, and Breaking Away from Perfectionism. As I stated, I have not read it yet, but I am going to and what I got from the titles where amazing. The chapter on excess baggage; where can you put them is a book all by itself. Excess means extra and baggage is the things we carry around, and I've had excess baggage in my life that held me down too long and I put them in the hands of someone I knew could handle them; God. I gave it all to Him; He tells me when I am weak, He is strong. That is why I love Him so much. Then the chapter on breaking away from perfectionism made me smile because the Holy Bible says that we all have sinned and came short of the glory of God, and one without sin cast the first stone. We all have some things in our lives that we are not happy with or need fixing, because we strive to be perfect but we will never be. There is only one perfect and that is God above. When I hear the word breaking away, I think of no more chains holding me. I am free at last. I never thought that I would be content as I am now with life because of what I had been through in my life. That is the one purpose of my book is to let it be testimony to those going through. The Lord knows all and He will never put more on us then we can bear. When we go through life and we have trials and tribulations, they are only tests to shape and mold us into the people that God intended for us to become one day. I am happy that God looks beyond our faults and see our needs. My book is my testimony. I may not be able to reach everyone in the world, but my book will travel and people will know that God will bring them through. No matter what you are going through, where you come from, and where you are going, God is that navigation system you will always need to keep handy. He told me a long time ago that He would never leave or forsake me. I believed it then but more now than ever. He kept His loving arms of protection around me even when the devil tried to take my joy. God made me and He knew that I was not made to break. He knew that the difficulties of my life would only make me stronger and wiser. I am thankful that even though I did not have my mother or father around growing up, He stepped in and was all that and more. I love my parents and I thank God for giving me to them no matter the circumstances. I love you Lord because you first loved me even when I did not think I could love myself. This is all a testimony is; a test to see if you can handle life when it throws you a curve ball that makes you wants to shrivel up and die. I was in that state of mind one time, but God brought me through and if you trust and believe in Him, He will do the same for you too. He said that He has no respectable person. This is my testimony in my life story format, and I pray that after you have read my book, that you know that life is full of tests, lies, disappointments, and some unhappiness, but it is solely left up to you to take God at His word. Take that stand and say to life peace be still. After taking a trip down memory lane and taking back what the devil thought he stole from, I realize that Life Lies turned into Love and Happiness.

Printed in the United States
By Bookmasters